Brave Empathy
A Feelings Field Guide

By Deborah Woods, National Board-Certified Counselor

PLAYTIME BAY PUBLISHING

Courageous Gratitude: Celebrate Your Journey Through Motherhood
(Playtime Presence Series, Book 1)

Brave Empathy (Playtime Presence Series, Book 2)

Courageous Gratitude: Celebrate Fatherhood
(Playtime Presence Series, Book 3)

This book is the second in the Playtime Presence Series.

For more information on the next book in this series, you can contact the author, Deborah Woods, NCC at her email address Deborah@deborahwoodsncc.com

Copyright © 2019 by Deborah Woods
ISBN-13: 978-0-578-45595-2 (Playtime Bay Publishing)

All Rights Reserved. This reservation of rights includes the right to reproduce this in whole or in part, to store it in digital or other formats, and/or to reproduce it in other forms and formats, including in pictures, photos or other ways of depicting any or all, of the material in here. No part of this may be reproduced, distributed or made available in any form, nor may it be stored or made available in any type of database or retrieval system except with written permission of the copyright owner.

If you are interested in using some of what I wrote or to make it available in some way, please contact me so we can explore that. I can be contacted at: Deborah@deborahwoodsncc.com

Protecting copyright is a powerful way to show your support while acknowledging in gratitude the work that took months to complete and ensuring that it can be made available. Thank you!

I hope this book encourages you to explore, to notice and name, to mention and appreciate, your emotions. I hope it inspires you to bravery and courage, when you see your children, your friends and family, and your co-workers, having feelings.

 I hope it minimizes the misunderstandings, casts off the burden of stoicism, and inspires patience and connection. I hope this book inspires you to see new possibilities in yourself, in your children, and in your world.

This book is educational information only. It's not advice. No therapeutic advice is being given and no therapist/patient, or counselor/client relationship is created.

I invite you to join me on this journey. Discover the adventures of brave empathy.

Dedication

This book is dedicated to my husband, David, who has loved me faithfully throughout all the comfortable and uncomfortable feelings. We are Team Woods.

Table of Contents

Chapter 1: Brave the Feelings 2

Chapter 2: What is Empathy? 18

Chapter 3: The Purpose of Feelings 30

Chapter 4: The Role of Compassion 42

Chapter 5: Savor Comfortable Feelings 64

Chapter 6: Sympathy 78

Chapter 7: Kids and Empathy 90

Chapter 8: Adjust Uncomfortable Feelings 106

Brave Empathy

Chapter 1: Brave the Feelings

Did your mother gather you up in her arms and kiss away your boo-boos? Did she look at you with disgust and threaten to give you something to cry about if you kept crying? Perhaps, she did a combination of these things depending on how stressed she was at the time. Either way, you learned the way to handle uncomfortable feelings is to make them go away. The faster, the better.

Makes sense. After all, who wants to feel uncomfortable? The trouble is, in all this hurry to get rid of uncomfortable feelings, we miss the mark. In the natural desire to avoid the pain, the icky-ness of it all, we miss some BIG critically important things about life, love, and the experience of being human.

Hold up. Did I just say don't kiss away your child's boo-boos? Before, you toss this book in the trash and decide what I'm saying is complete rubbish, let me explain. I personally love to have my boo-boos kissed and comforted with soothing tones and reassurances that I am loved.

The question remains, is avoidance the best way to BE human, to live and to flourish? Is it the best way to operate a body and mind equipped with a complicated set of emotions, a standard feature, built into every human being? Or is there a better way?

Whether we like it or not, feelings aren't a luxury feature we can refuse. Whether we want them or not, everyone has feelings. The real question is, how do we deal with these pesky little critters? What's wrong with the status quo? Why can't we just keep avoiding them like we have been? Can't we just keep the comfortable ones and toss out the uncomfortable ones?

In this book, we're going to explore the realm of human emotions, some comfortable and delightful, others uncomfortable and raw. I'm going to introduce you to the concept of BRAVE EMPATHY. We'll explore what it means to experience brave empathy and how to use it to connect with others. You'll discover the rich variety of feelings that make up the landscape of human existence, from the moment we're born until the moment we cease to be. You'll find out how to spot a bunch of those different feelings and call them by name to make them less strange and unfamiliar. When we get familiar enough with the landmarks, those feelings aren't near as likely to frighten us away.

Have you ever been so annoyed by someone's feelings that you just wanted to shut them up?

Brave Empathy

Have you wanted to make someone stop all that uncomfortable thing they're doing that makes you feel so uncomfortable?

Getting familiar with the realm of human emotions and mastering the art and science of brave empathy will enable you to show up and be brave enough to withstand the feelings of others without feeling compelled to shut them up.

The brave in brave empathy is not a feeling. It's a choice, an attitude, an act of will. We may feel brave, at times, but something I've noticed about feeling brave is that the feeling usually comes after I take actions that I believe are brave. When it comes to being brave, action comes before feeling. That's how it is with brave empathy.

I make a choice to notice and accept someone's uncomfortable feeling, without rushing to change it. I bravely tolerate my own discomfort while I notice and identify the feeling. Familiarity makes being brave easier. After a while, it seems natural. In the pages that follow, you'll discover how to navigate through the complex range of emotions that accompany the human experience.

You'll be relieved to discover that feelings are temporary. They come, and they go. Whether it's a feeling of exuberant joy we want to hang onto forever or the heartbreaking grief we want to avoid all together, when these feelings come, they also pass. Feelings, even though they're always with us, are also constantly changing. Like the sights we see from the car as we pass them along the road as we go driving by, feelings are temporary. Still, you can be certain there are always more on the road ahead. Feelings are unavoidable.

Human connection happens when we share our thoughts, feelings, and experiences. The ability to be present, to tolerate and stay with someone who is sharing an uncomfortable feeling is a vital element of human connection. Without the ability to tolerate the uncomfortable feelings of others, we will rush to shutting them down. We will disconnect. In that disconnection, we create new feelings of isolation and loneliness that compound the painful experience. Connection enables us to move through the uncomfortable feelings, to help them heal and pass, as we move on to more comfortable feelings. Brave empathy equips us to remain present, to tolerate our own discomfort without shutting down our compassion.

Come on in. Keep reading. You'll see what I mean.

Let's start by looking at a roadmap of where I'm going to be taking you. I want to give you the lay of the land to help you enjoy the sights along the way and get the most out of our tour through the realm of human emotion. As you flip through the pages, you'll notice feeling words and definitions, much like a dictionary. I've included examples along with each of the definitions to help you get a more panoramic view.

The stories include thoughts, feelings, and behaviors to help you recognize each feeling in revealing detail. We'll look at a mixture of comfortable and uncomfortable feelings, moving from comfortable to uncomfortable at a predictable rhythm. Unfortunately, our emotions aren't quite as predictable although they are as fluid and changing. You'll discover, beautiful photos accompanying the comfortable feelings, adding a visual element to enhance your understanding and experience of that emotion while we're there.

When we come to the uncomfortable feelings, you'll discover that instead of selecting photos that evoke unpleasant sensations, I've selected photos that help ease the discomfort. My goal is not to take you so deep into the uncomfortable feelings that you toss the book aside but rather to enable you to regulate and adjust your emotional discomfort as you go along. In this way, you'll find that you can maintain your interest and motivation, even during the more difficult ground.

This is where you will need to reach inside yourself and pull out some bravery. You will inevitably see something that reminds you of an uncomfortable feeling you've experienced. If not in the story itself, perhaps as you're thinking about the writing prompt. I've included the prompts to help you explore your experience of each feeling. The strong tides and challenging terrain are worth braving for the chance to spot a fiery feeling hiding in the underbrush.

Take the journal prompts at your own pace. No need to rush these. Do what you like and leave the rest until you're ready to explore those further. Every few pages, there'll be a place to pause and reflect, to rest from the changing rhythm of emotions. In these pages, I'll reveal more about brave empathy and what it is and how to have more of it.

Enjoy the journey. I'll be here with you every step of the way.

Brave Empathy

The mothering part of my journey began when I was waiting for the birth of my son. I felt confident that I knew how to be a good mom. In college, I'd studied child psychology and child development. I felt prepared to be a mom. I was sure my child would be happy and well adjusted.

UNTIL my son was born. Suddenly, I discovered being a mom was much harder than I ever thought possible. I wasn't prepared for what I was up against.

The challenges my husband and I faced stressed our marriage nearly to the breaking point. I was trained as a professional counselor, to help kids with their feelings. Yet, my son's behavior at home and at school had me riding a painful roller coaster of uncomfortable and challenging emotions.

Today, I'm proud of the man my son has grown into. He's overcome learning disabilities and anxiety. He's developed great people skills. He's well liked and successful at work. He's happily married and celebrating a wedding anniversary soon. We all have a close and loving relationship. He seeks my advice when he needs it. He's strong and independent and capable. I'm proud of how I raised him. Instead of crying myself to sleep these days, I cry tears of joy remembering how far we've come.

Hi, I'm Deborah Woods, National Board-Certified Counselor. I feel a deep sense of satisfaction knowing the things my son, my husband, and I struggled with has helped so many other moms, dads, grandparents, and kids avoid the years of pain and frustration we suffered.

Since we're going to be spending some time in this book exploring a wide range of comfortable and uncomfortable emotions, let's stop a moment and define what I mean by an emotion.

An emotion is a natural instinctive reaction; a feeling; a state of mind deriving from one's circumstances, point of view, or relationships, typically accompanied by physiological changes in the body that show up as changes in behavior.

That's quite a mouth full. Let me break it down a bit. An emotion is a natural reaction to something that happens combined with our thoughts about the thing that happened. We experience a change in the sensations in our bodies and react by changing what we do.

For example, we hear a mother singing a lullaby to her baby. Then, in a split second, we might think about how sweet it is and perhaps even remember our own mother singing a lullaby to us. We feel a change in our bodies. Our breathing slows as we enjoy the mother's song. The muscle tension goes out of our hands and they gently open. We sink into the chair and notice that we're feeling relaxed.

On the other hand, for those of us who had a more painful relationship with our mothers, the sight and sounds of a mother singing a lullaby to her baby awaken other thoughts and feelings. Perhaps, a deep longing and sense of loss stirs within us. Tears form in our eyes. Our bodies tense. We feel saddened and turn away.

Our emotional reactions are as unique and varied as we are. The experiences that have shaped our emotional landscape is all our own. No other person has experienced life exactly as we have.

You may have experienced some feelings that are like feelings I've experienced. You may have had some feelings I've not had. Either way, as I reach out to share with you and you lean in to listen, we connect. Brené Brown defines connection as the energy that exists between two people when they feel seen, heard, and valued; when they give and receive without judgment; and when they derive sustenance and strength from the relationship.

Sadly, instead of feeling connected, our emotional reactions sometimes leave us feeling disconnected and in conflict with the people who matter most to us. For parents, emotions can create an especially big challenge.

Kids feel things, intensely, deeply, and loudly at times. Given that fact, it's disappointing that kids don't come fully equipped with what it takes to mention and manage feelings in a way that leaves us feeling connected.

Riding the roller coaster of a child's moods can be brutal.

By the way, that BEHAVIOR, it's coming from a feeling. I find that many people simply aren't aware that behavior is an indication of a feeling. When you see someone, a child, a spouse, a co-worker, or friend, doing that thing or saying those words and you wonder, "What in the world is going on?" They're having a feeling, probably a strong one. If you're seeing them act out in ways that are surprising, there's a good chance they're having difficulty using that feeling in a way that is helpful.

Both kids and parents need help figuring out what to do with the constant barrage of feelings that pop up in unexpected corners all throughout the day. Knowing what to do with our own feelings is one thing. The added pressure of having to help our kids with theirs can be overwhelming.

Conventional ways of reacting to a child's emotions, like time-out, grounding, star charts, and taking away privileges, leave kids unprepared to understand and share his emotions. These strategies leave kids disconnected and conflict, without the skills to resolve the conflict or to repair relationship. Parents often discover the fight that goes into getting kids into time out or the argument over the loss of privileges provokes more conflict, anger, and resentment. Before long, parents and kids are caught up in a struggle over who has the power in the relationship.

A while back I did a Google search of "I hate being a mother." The search produced so many pages of results, I had to stop reading after a few hours. I was struck by the huge numbers of mothers anonymously posting their agony. Mother after mother was posting about her frustration with being a mom. Mom after mom wrote comments like this one:

> "My kids fight, scream, and demand all the time. I am so unhappy. No one tells you how awful it is to be a mother. No one! Yes, there are little sweet things that happen from time to time but, over all, it's terrible. I am so exhausted that I can't sleep at night. My nerves are shot from the kids constant yelling, fighting, and having to explain, soothe, or whatever 24/7. I love my kids, but I hate being a mom."

Like most of the moms posting, this mom feels overwhelmed and exhausted. Her kids are feeling irritable, demanding, and unsatisfied. Most of the comments left by those who found her rant online and others like hers are without compassion. Empathy for the plight of these moms was rare in the comments that I read. It was heartbreaking to read.

Maybe you're like some parents who have compliant, easy to live with children who keep their feelings to themselves and rarely act out. Maybe you have a child who withdraws when he's overwhelmed by his emotions. Maybe you have a child whose life experiences challenge them beyond their ability to cope leaving you to pick up the pieces. Perhaps, you even have a combination of these different little people in your home. Regardless, I'm certain you'll find brave empathy a valuable tool to keep tucked into your backpack on your journey together.

Look over the definitions and stories. Consider the writing prompts. Pay attention to the sensations you experience and the ways you react to your emotions

Notice your child's behavior. Get curious about what your child might be feeling.

As we explore the hills and valleys together, I'd like to invite you to stop in at my Facebook group: Play Connect Influence. Ask a question. Post a comment about what you're noticing.

I'd love to hear about your experiences and support you in your growth. You'll find the Facebook group at: https://www.facebook.com/groups/playconnect/

Brave Empathy

Accepted — liked; seen as good, normal, pleasing, chosen; feeling you are part of the group; received, welcomed, identified and recognized as a group member.

Accepting — open; valuing someone else; offering a good opinion of; showing respect and approval for someone as a member of your group.

"ARRR! I'll get you with my sharp teeth now," Logan snarls with enthusiasm. He moves in to attack again. His dad, James, smiles as he holds Logan's prey still, while Logan eagerly pokes and presses his assault. "Should I make it easy or hard for him to get me?" James whispers to Logan. James defers to Logan. James wants Logan to experience his respect for him and his ideas. James sees Logan's need to express his feelings of strength and power and sacrifices his impulse to thrash Logan's dinosaur. Logan moves in closer to his dad. Logan feels accepted as James follows his lead and plays in the ways Logan wants to play. They both feel a sense of belonging. James and Logan feel accepted and accepting.

Logan's mom, Amy notices she's interested in the other moms in her moms' group. She's curious about their opinions and interests. As she offers to make coffee, she's aware that she's trying to meet their needs even when it's not convenient. Amy remembers how she stays a little longer than she expected at the meetings and offers to help clean up after the meeting even though she's got a busy schedule. She's comfortable sharing her hopes and dreams when she's with the other moms in the group because she feels safe and content in their company. Considering all this, Amy realizes, she feels accepted and accepting.

When have you felt accepted? Accepting?

Brave Empathy

Rejected — feeling that one is refused, cast away, and not welcome; feeling that others see you as not good enough; not being welcome, accepted or allowed into the group.

Disapproving — to withhold acceptance or approval; to have an unfavorable, critical, hostile, or negative opinion.

Riley approached two of her friends, Hunter and Danielle. They were engrossed in conversation. She waited patiently for them to finish their conversation and acknowledge her. To her surprise, when they finished talking, the two of them turned and went their separate ways leaving her standing there alone. Riley hung her head. Her shoulders sunk as she let out an involuntary whimper. Riley felt rejected.

Danielle feigned interest for as long as she could. Hunter told Danielle all about her latest crush on the new boy at school. Danielle thought about the countless other crushes Hunter had that year and how quickly each of those had faded. Danielle, bit her lip to avoid saying something sarcastic, rolled her eyes, and walked away. Danielle felt disapproving.

When did you feel rejected?

When you felt disapproving, how did you show it?

Brave Empathy

Bubbly — enthusiastic, lively, talkative, positive, excited.

Cheerful — noticeably happy and optimistic; full of pleasant, sunny, eager attitude.

Charlotte's eyes danced as she raised her scepter to pronounce the decree that all her kingdom was to celebrate. She commanded that everyone exchange compliments and gifts, and then, skip around in the streets. All her made-up subjects scurried around happily complying with her wishes. She ordered that they tell jokes and laugh loudly. Their imagined laughter filled her heart. Her face glowed with delight. She waved her stick with enthusiasm as she spoke. "I wish I could hug the whole world," Charlotte exclaimed. Charlotte was feeling bubbly and cheerful.

Can you recall a time when you felt bubbly or cheerful?

How could you recapture that feeling?

Brave Empathy

Gloomy – dark or dim; depressed; sad; hopeless, despairing or pessimistic.

Grieved – feelings of great sorrow and distress at the loss of something or someone; mourning.

Gwen's eyes looked red. Her eyes were puffy. She'd been crying. Her eye makeup was smeared. Her chin trembled whenever someone asked her about her mother's latest trip to the hospital. When she recalled the words of the doctor, she couldn't remember anything good he'd said. She just kept thinking about how she'd lost her dad the year before. She bent forward and laid her head on her arms. Gwen felt gloomy and grieved.

When did you feel gloomy?

What helps you to cope with feelings of grief?

Brave Empathy

Chapter 2: What is Empathy?

Empathy is a word that gets thrown around quite a bit these days, usually without defining what it is. We generally accept the idea that we should have empathy for one another, but few of us are clear on exactly what that means. Different people use the word empathy to mean different things.

Here's what I mean by EMPATHY: Empathy is being aware of and able to accurately identify the feelings of another. Empathy has two important elements. First, the awareness and ability to recognize when others are experiencing feelings and secondly, the ability to identify those feelings with a degree of accuracy. Both are critical components of empathy.

For example, empathy is hearing my son talk about a project he's working on and noticing his smile and the enthusiasm in his voice. He commented, "Can you believe it, Mom?"

I noticed he was having a feeling by the smile on his face and the sound of his voice. Using what he's said and what I saw, I can make an educated guess that he's most likely feeling proud of himself. It's not a big leap from what I see and hear to guessing that he's feeling proud.

Empathy is NOT the feeling of pride that wells up inside me when I hear him talking about how well he's doing on the project. My feeling of pride for him, is not the same as his feelings of pride in himself. His feelings of pride in himself may trigger my feelings of pride for him but we are separate people and his feelings are not mine. He has his own experience that is separate from mine.

I remind myself to listen to him and to stay curious about what his experience is like, knowing that it is likely different from my own experience of enthusiasm and pride.

It's helpful to remember that I could be entirely wrong about what I think he's feeling. Even if I am highly accurate much of the time, when I'm identifying what feelings I see in others, I know, I could get it wrong. The process of being aware and identifying feelings is guesswork at best. Practicing empathy requires that I accept the inevitable fact that at some point I will guess inaccurately. I could get it wrong.

Responding with empathy can look like, "I see you smiling as you're telling me about your work. You sound so enthusiastic. I imagine you're feeling really proud." Most days, if I sound natural and caring in my response, he'll tilt his head and pause. Then he'll add, "Yeah. I am feeling proud of myself."

Brave Empathy

There's a chance, however, that even if I call it right, I could be aware of and identify a feeling that he hasn't become aware of yet himself. If he's not yet aware of it he might respond, "No, I don't really care that much about it. I just think it's an interesting project."

Of course, there's the possibility that I missed the identification entirely and he's not feeling proud. He could be feeling excited to get to work with a mentor he's excited to learn more from.

Either way, my efforts to notice his feelings and identify them as accurately as possible, increased the connection between us. He doesn't need 100% accuracy. He needs my brave attempt to stay present and interested in him and his feelings.

Empathy is an imaginative act of stepping into the shoes of another person and attempting to get a glimpse of the world from their perspective. It requires being curious and wanting to understand the feelings, beliefs, hopes and experiences that make up another's interpretation of the world.
At the same time, empathy involves accepting that we can never fully know what it's like to be another person, living in their skin and experiencing the things they've experienced.

This desire to be open and aware, to identify as much as possible, and to accept that we cannot fully know requires bravery on our part. It takes courage to remain open, to continue attempting to identify, risking we could miss our goal and end up being told we're wrong, even if we properly read all the cues and made a great guess.

Brave empathy involves choosing to be sincerely concerned and curious about the struggles of another instead of discounting their discomfort. Brave empathy reveals that we care enough to make the effort and risk being vulnerable.

Brave empathy is aided by a strong feeling word vocabulary. Being able to recognize and identify feelings is easier when you have a rich vocabulary you can use to distinguish one emotional state from another. By "feeling word" I mean the name by which a feeling or emotion is known. Happy, sad, scared and mad are all feeling words that describe different emotional states.

Sometimes I get startled by a sudden loud noise. When I get startled, I've been known to let out an involuntary scream. After I comment, "Wow, that surprised me!" Surprised is a feeling word. When I use feeling words, I'm modeling expressing my emotions with feeling words.

Brené Brown in *Dare to Lead*, says that we need to be able to easily recognize and identify between 30 to 40 emotions in ourselves and others to be what she calls "emotionally fluent." Because we're constantly feeling something, emotional fluency helps relationships run more smoothly.

Couples therapist and author, Brian Gleason, says that "emotional fluency" primes cooperation while "disfluency" primes conflict. The ability to identify and put into words the emotions that fill my internal experiences, my inner world, enable me to create harmony and cooperation in my relationships, whether those relationships are with my husband, my son, or the people with whom I work.

If parents want kids to express feelings with words, instead of acting out, the best thing they can do is to use feeling words themselves. Modeling is more powerful than telling.

Without a rich feeling word vocabulary, it's hard to express the full range of human emotions. Kids who grow up without being exposed to a rich feeling word vocabulary become adults who are limited to describing emotions as good or bad; alright or mad. They have trouble understanding and expressing what they're experiencing.

People with great people skills are able to use their rich feeling word vocabulary to connect with others. Adults who identify all uncomfortable emotions as anger, find it hard to relate to the feelings of others. They misinterpret the motivations of their friends and family. They get defensive and aggressive because they wrongly assume their co-workers are angry.

Without a broad understanding of emotions, it's hard to have empathy. Empathy requires a person be able to recognize and identify a wide range of emotions. Emotional fluency can and must be learned.

As you begin noticing and identifying your feelings, try to use these feeling words in casual conversation. As you do, you're modeling emotional fluency. You're enriching your child's feeling word vocabulary and you're building your own.

Brave Empathy

Peaceful – calm, quiet, restful; seeking to stay away from conflict or excitement, free from disturbance, agitation, or strife.

Satisfied – having desires, needs, or expectations met; content, pleased, fulfilled.

Paul stretched out on the grass and leaned back resting his head in his hands, savoring the moment. He took a deep, contented breath as he smiled at his mom. Paul commented on about how much he enjoyed their picnic in the park together. His voice was warm and caring. "I could stay here with you forever," he told his mom, Sandy. Paul felt peaceful and satisfied.

Sandy felt a sensation of warmth spread throughout her body as if the sun had suddenly decided to shine a bit brighter. A sudden thought, that all the forces of hatred and violence had been vanquished and the world peace she'd dreamed of was finally a reality, formed in her imagination. She settled herself next to Paul on the grass for a well-deserved rest. Sandy felt peaceful and satisfied.

When have you felt peaceful?

Do you recall a time when you felt satisfied?

Dissatisfied – unhappy or displeased with something or someone; arising from the belief that something isn't as good as it should be.

Resigned – willingly having accepted, without complaining, something unpleasant that one cannot do anything about; to give up without resistance.

Once again, Ray found himself agreeing with his brother Dylan, only to avoid an argument. Ray assumed Dylan would be disappointed and feel let down if he told Dylan what he really thought. Ray was tired. He felt a painful lump in his throat. His arms and legs felt too heavy to move. He told himself that it was no use. "Dylan and I will always disagree," Ray said out loud to no one in particular. Ray felt resigned.

Dylan collapsed into his chair. He heaved a heavy sigh and covered his face with his hands as he tried to hide his face. He cursed under his breath, berating himself for how he spoke to his brother just moments earlier. His chest felt tight as he thought about all the things that he wished he would have said but didn't. Dylan felt dissatisfied.

How would you complete these sentences? I felt dissatisfied when …

I felt resigned when …

Assertive – characterized by brave or self-assured statements and behavior; expresses one's feelings, needs, desires, thoughts and opinions clearly, so others take notice.

Confident – sure of oneself; believing in one's own abilities; showing independence; being certain of something; aware of one's powers and strengths.

Ava is calm and focused as she picks up her tools and pretends to work. After playing with the tools for a while, she looks her mother directly in the eye. "I'm fixing the house for you, Mom. I'm good at this." Ava gives her mom, Connie, a playful grin. Ava continues to work with the tools. Connie comes closer to get a better look. Comfortable with moms' presence, Ava pats her hat and tells her mom that she's got a hat. Connie responds, "I see you have your hat right there on your head." Ava hands her mom a toy tool from her toolbox and directs Connie to work on fixing a dollhouse. Connie follows Ava's lead. She notices that Ava is feeling assertive and confident.

I feel confident when …

I feel assertive when …

Brave Empathy

Aggressive – ready or likely to attack or confront; combative; making an all-out effort to win or succeed; using force to convince.

Anxious – feeling worry, unease, or nervousness, typically about an approaching event or something with an uncertain outcome; characterized by dwelling on fear about some possibility.

Alan's nostrils flared. His eyes hardened. Public Defender, Alan, stomped into the courthouse where he was planning to confront the prosecuting attorney. He rushed past the judge's office with a full head of steam. Alan looked like he was ready for a fight. His heart raced. His body was tense. Alan was feeling aggressive.

Adam looked over at the clock for the third time in the last 15 minutes. It seemed to him like time had slowed to a snail's pace. He shifted in his seat, unable to get comfortable. He pulled at his shirt as if it were scratching him. It was his first time in a counselor's office, and he had no idea what was expected of him. Adam was feeling anxious.

A time I felt aggressive was …

A time I felt anxious was …

Brave Empathy

Chapter 3: The Purpose of Feelings

There are hundreds of words that refer to the various shades and intensities of emotions and feelings. You may be relieved to hear I've limited our tour to just 80 instead of hundreds. I'm convinced I've felt a high percentage of the possible range of emotions during my lifetime. I imagine you have too.

There were times when it seemed like an avalanche of emotion had me trapped under its suffocating weight. I wondered, "Why do I have all these feelings?" I wondered, "What would happen if I ignored, avoided, or discounted all my uncomfortable emotions and experiences? I asked myself, "Can't I just NOT feel?"

Unfortunately, NOT feeling, is a feeling. It's called feeling numb. After a while, I discovered that even feeling numb is uncomfortable.

Then, I realized, feelings have a purpose. Even the uncomfortable feelings I was experiencing, had a valuable purpose. Feelings serve as powerful motivators. My feelings gave me useful information. They alerted me to dangers and unmet needs. They inform me about what I want to hold onto and make more of in my life. Even when feelings are confusing, they're an important piece of the puzzle to understand ourselves and others.

It was a long expedition to discover the importance of recognizing and identifying my feelings. It took a lot of courage to trek through the cold and dark places where my hidden emotions had been buried. Like many people, I grew up in a family where feelings were brushed aside, pushed down, and buried for generations. It seemed to me that feelings were dangerous. Having a feeling, expressing a feeling, resulted in conflict, rejection, and even attack and injury.

I sat in the dark bedroom, where curtains blocked the summer sun, feeling sad and lonely. I'd just turned thirteen and I missed my home in Southern California. My family had recently moved to a farm in rural Missouri. Everything in the country was unfamiliar and thorny.

I was a city girl. I didn't know anything about coping with outdoor toilets and snakes in the yard between the house and the toilet. I couldn't understand why anyone would want to live that way on purpose. Moving had meant leaving behind my best friend, my grandparents, and all that I called HOME.

Brave Empathy

My dad came into my room and sat next to me. I wanted to talk to him about what was on my mind that day, what I was feeling. What I didn't know was how afraid of my feelings my dad was.

He had always seemed powerful to me. I had never seen him out of control or overwhelmed by emotion. He was strong and silent about everything but his passion for his work. Seeing me dissolve into tears, brought on a parade of his own fears and he reacted by walking out on me. He left me sitting there crying without a word. I felt rejected and alone. I was completely baffled by his reaction.

Now looking back on his life, his behavior makes sense. No one ever told him that his feelings mattered. His mother died when he was a small boy. His father numbed his grief with alcohol. There wasn't anyone noticing that my dad was having feelings of any kind. It makes sense that he didn't have the skillset to notice and identify my feelings. He couldn't respond with empathy when he had no base of knowledge on which to build empathy skills.

He was doing the best he knew how to do. Sadly, his best was inadequate for the task of raising a teenage daughter who like him, had lost her mother. My dad had a whole pile of big feelings that he didn't talk openly about. He never talked about losing my mother to schizophrenia and all he went through in his marriage to her. He never talked about the pain of losing his own mother. He never talked about what it was like growing up in the care of a grieving alcoholic father.

Yet, I saw the sadness in his face. I noticed without knowing what I was seeing. Years later, I discovered all those feelings have names. Without names for my feelings, I had no idea how to talk to him about them. I suspect he may have felt the same.

My loneliness motivated me to search for connection. Confusion motivated me to seek out an understanding of emotions. I dug deep and discovered that anger motivates us to change or fix something that is not working. Anger gives us the strength, energy and power to stand up against an injustice. Sometimes, we use anger to protect us from hurt and sadness.

I found that sadness helps us reflect on the significance of something we've have lost, or something that has disappointed us. When we feel sad, it's natural to want to be alone. Withdrawing, when we're sad, protects us from getting further hurt until we feel stronger. Sadness lets others see that we need comforting.

Fear protects you from unsafe risks and tells you to be careful or to prepare to flee an unsafe situation. Fear is natural in unfamiliar situations.

Comfortable feelings tell you what's working. Joy alerts our brains to pay special attention to these extraordinary feelings and motivates us to re-create the conditions where feelings of contentment, satisfaction, happiness, peace and joy happen. Comfortable feelings say, "Do that again." Joy renews my hope. Gratitude refreshes me. Playfulness energizes me and strengthens me to bounce back from stress.

Finally, I realized that feelings are beneficial. Comfortable or uncomfortable, I benefit from having feelings. Life is better with feelings than it is without them. Feelings make my experience of life richer and fuller. I'm grateful for all my feelings.

These discoveries prepared me to help my son navigate through the full range of emotions that he encountered as he grew from a baby into the man he is today.

Empathy is one of the tools I used to break the generational cycle into which I was born. I no longer try to avoid my feelings, comfortable or uncomfortable. I learn from them and use them to enrich my life and to inspire others. I have passed this important skill down to my son.

This is the gift I give you today. Use it well and it will change your life.

Brave Empathy

Curious – eager to know or learn; desiring to investigate; having an inquisitive interest; enquiring.

Adventurous – willing to take risks or to try out new, unusual, and exciting methods, ideas, or experiences.

Kenayah paused to examine the bug crawling in the weeds she'd been kicking. She bent down to get a closer look through her magnifying glass. A slow smile formed on her face as she studied the bug's shape. "Look at this," she exclaimed, "Just look at it. It's awesome. What do you think it is?" She edged closer and closer hoping to get a clue as to what kind of bug it was. Kenayah felt curious.

Jamie leaned forward to see what Kenayah was studying. Jamie's eyes were wide as she stared at the bug Kenayah had discovered. Losing all her usual inhibitions, Jamie reached out and picked the bug up to have a closer look. Jamie was feeling adventurous.

When have you felt curious?

Do you recall a time when you felt adventurous? What happened?

Brave Empathy

Bored – uninterested in one's current activity; feeling unstimulated; having nothing to occupy one's time; experiences a situation as dull.

Guarded – cautious, having hesitations, concerns or misgivings; careful; restrained; careful not to show feelings or give away information.

Brad shrugged his shoulders half-heartedly. He wandered around the room staring vacantly at the objects in view. His only words were an occasional, "Yeah." He sat down, slumped himself into the chair, and started to pick lint off his sweater. Occasionally he'd yawn. Brad closed his eyes to shut out the world around him as he waited. Brad was feeling bored.

Georgia tried to maintain an even tone in her voice. She offered a fake smile. She forced herself to stay calm. When her ex-husband and his new wife laughed, Georgia forced out a laugh. She tried changing the subject but was unsuccessful. She didn't want another argument over what was best for the kids. When she couldn't avoid the issue, she tried to reason her point with facts and logic. She knew she'd get nowhere if she allowed herself to get swept up in an emotional debate. She sifted her memories for evidence to support her point of view. Georgia felt guarded.

How do you show when you're feeling bored?

When have you felt guarded?

Brave Empathy

Loved – looked upon with deep affection; cherished; held dear; wanted; considered with tenderness.

Loving – feeling or showing love, care or concern; tender and kind affection, fondness and warmth.

Luke snuggled up against his dad, Leo. Leo leaned in close to Luke. Luke's eyes sparkled as he smiled. Leo got close to Luke's ear and whispered, "Don't tell anyone, but you're my favorite buddy, Luke." Luke giggled as he enjoyed the closeness. He reached up and felt his dad's face. "Dad, I like your mustache. I hope I get a mustache like yours when I get to be big like you." Luke and Leo are feeling loved and loving.

Describe a time when you felt loved.

When did you feel loving? How did you show it?

Brave Empathy

Forgotten – no longer remembered or thought about; unnoticed; disregarded; abandoned; given over to obscurity.

Withdrawn – refusing or not wanting to communicate; removed from community, and relationships; socially detached, disconnected and unresponsive; isolated.

Fiona pinched her lips together tightly to keep them from trembling. A painful tightness welled up in her throat. She fought back the urge to run away as she choked back tears. Ever since her best friend, Wren, had left for summer camp, the house next door had become a painful reminder of how Fiona had been left behind. She wanted to be happy for Wren but the thought that Wren had betrayed her by going to camp without her kept swirling in her head. Fiona couldn't help but imagine what great fun Wren was having without her. She hoped Wren would miss her but had convinced herself that Wren hadn't even given her a single thought the whole time. Fiona guessed Wren would never want her as a best friend again after all the new friends she was making at camp. Fiona felt forgotten.

When Wren returned from summer camp, Fiona turned down Wren's invitations to hang out, making up excuses to put Wren off. Fiona dreaded hearing about Wren's new friends. When they rode the bus to school, Fiona pretended to read a book to avoid talking to Wren. When Wren tried to engage her in conversation, Fiona turned away and went back to reading after muttering a quick deadpan, "That's nice." Fiona feels withdrawn.

When have you felt forgotten or withdrawn? How did you cope with those feelings?

Chapter 4: The Role of Compassion

Feelings are complicated. I find the rarest sunken treasures in the murkiest waters. The deep dive yields surprising discoveries. Here's a gem I found in a vulnerable place where my husband and I shared an uncomfortable conflict. He suggested I share it with you.

My husband, David, felt angry after I said something to him, that to me, felt like an innocent remark. His reaction stunned me. Later in the day, a similar thing happened. I said something, spontaneously sharing my thoughts and feelings, in an enthusiastic desire to connect and explore a need, but he felt offended and withdrew into silence.

Did I hurt his feelings? Did I make him mad at me? Did I cause him to retreat into silence? Did I set him off and cause the angry outburst that followed my words? Did it matter that he misunderstood my words and my intent? Did it matter that he misread my tone of voice and facial expressions?

Whose fault was it that we were in this uncomfortable conflict?

I felt completely innocent. It couldn't be my fault. What could be wrong with what I said?

He felt hurt and offended. He felt like the victim in the conflict. It couldn't be his fault.

Still, it had to be someone's fault and since I was the one who said the things that resulted in his feeling hurt, it must be my fault. He wanted an apology.

I didn't feel sorry. What was I supposed to apologize for? Why should I take the blame? If he wanted to blame someone, then it was his own fault that he twisted my words. He's the one who gave them some hurtful meaning I didn't intend for them to have. The way I saw it, his angry reaction had been far more malicious than my words. I believed I was the injured party. He had it all wrong. He owed me an apology for rudely and wrongly accusing me.

I imagined that if he'd understood my meaning and saw my good intentions, he would have said, "Oh Deborah, yes, I see what you mean. That's clever." He would have enjoyed my sense of humor and have smiled with me.

Emotions get complicated when one's piled on top of another. When he felt hurt, he also felt angry that I "never" apologize. I "always" claim to be innocent and misunderstood.

These are vast sweeping generalizations created in our minds to make sense of unresolved conflicts that reoccur over time. We create these to explain our feelings to ourselves. You may have heard these types of beliefs referred to as "story."

He "always" ends up as the bad guy who screwed things up. He "always" takes the blame and at the end of the argument, he's the one who apologizes. Even though he's the one who was hurt, he "never" gets the compassion and relationship repair that he needs to feel restored.

Writing this, I see his pain and feel compassion for him. I imagine he feels quite trapped. He's been a lawyer too long not to see the mound of evidence on his side. We've been married for thirty-eight and a half years. Add another four years for our college romance and you'll see that there's been plenty of time for these little conflicts to have created a pattern. Even at a rate of once a year, forty-two separate incidents could amount to a huge pile of evidence.

This is a classic example of why we need brave empathy. The huge pile of twisted stories and buried emotions tucked away in the recesses of our minds, can become a barricade around our hearts that choke out feelings of love and connection leaving distrust, loneliness, and even rage in its wake.

When he reacted, I didn't see his hurt. I saw his anger and felt defensive. I went straight to DEFCON 1 because his accusations that I "always" criticize him sparked a chain reaction in me. I felt threatened. If he thinks I'm always criticizing him, then he must think I'm a bad wife. I am not a bad wife. He should be grateful that I'm his wife and not some other woman who wouldn't put up with him. My thoughts swirl, trying to protect me, from this unwanted identity of "bad wife." His anger sparked my fears that I'm not good enough. The suggestion that he puts me together with the behavior of a "bad wife," left me feeling condemned. I protected myself by clinging to my belief that I am a "good wife." I vehemently protested that I was innocent.

Before you judge me, you might want to consider the possibility that you've gotten caught up in some of this type of thinking yourself. It would be normal if you've experienced something like this.

These are common mistakes humans make because we have rapidly changing emotions that operate behind the scenes, often on autopilot. The things I describe weren't things I was aware of in the moment.

It took a good twenty-four hours, including a good night's sleep, for me to find my feelings of compassion for him. Emotions are powerful little motivators that take some time to uncover.

What if, I had noticed his anger and remembered that I'm vulnerable to accusations that fuel my fears? What if I had reassured myself that while I am a "good wife," I do sometimes say things that can be experienced as hurtful.

What if, I had been curious about the way my words impacted my husband when I saw his anger? What if, I'd tried to imagine a time when I felt hurt by something I misunderstood?

What I noticed was that I did not feel compassion for him in his anger. In fact, I rarely feel compassion when his pain is expressed as anger. I interpret it as an attack and feel attacked. Then I feel defensive. He looks and sounds angry and hostile rather than hurt. I'm not moved to comfort him when he's blaming me for having hurt him in an angry tone of voice.

I see he's angry. I can't tell that he's hurt. It's much later that I realized he felt insulted. Yes, that's the word that accounts for his angry reaction and his hurt feelings. He believes I insulted him and was feeling hurt and angry.

Now, he makes sense to me but at the time, I just wanted him to see I did NOT set out to hurt him. It was an accident or a misunderstanding or some other strange occurrence but, I didn't mean to hurt him. I didn't deserve his angry reaction.

My defensive justifications felt to him like a sledge hammer. He experienced my defensive explanation as a condemnation that left him wishing he could go hide and cry. He wasn't feeling brave. He'd been through this dance too many times to hope for a different outcome. He felt unseen, unheard, and sad. He felt hopeless and so, he apologized to try to set things right again.

Thinking it through that next morning, I saw something new glistening down on the surface under the dark water.

Brave Empathy

He rarely gets comforted after he's been hurt.

I always thought these arguments were his own fault, that if he'd choose to see me for who I am, and not make up stories about what I meant, he wouldn't be hurt in the first place. If he'd just change his thinking, the whole problem would be solved.

I had missed the mark. I had failed to bring empathy.

Every time he apologized, I was more convinced of my innocence. I felt cleared of all charges. Except that I'm wasn't. He continued to believe that I had insulted him.

He had apologized for getting angry. I had accepted his apology. We had smoothed things over. We moved on without ever having resolved the conflict. Still, the hurt was not resolved. He felt trapped. He'd taken on all the blame and gotten no compassion. I walked away with no understanding of my part in the conflict. Because it was unresolved, this same argument happened over and over.

I firmly believe that what you do after what you did, makes a difference, because after what we did, we did something we do a lot. Something that keeps us happily married and devoted to one another. Something that has helped us resolve many conflicts over the years.

We worked together to find our empathy for one another.

I'd woken up that morning after the argument and discovered some compassion for him. He woke up willing to talk it out with me. I waited to hear his perspective first. Then, I shared mine and listened some more.

We talked about whether someone had to be at fault. Was it necessary that I admit that I insulted him when I didn't think I meant to insult him? We bravely listened and asked questions.

He helped me to see that I had used a word that to him meant something particularly offensive. I could see how what I said left him feeling insulted. He made sense to me. The impact he experienced wasn't the impact I was wanting when I spoke and yet, it was what he experienced. I regretted my choice of words. He acknowledged that I didn't deserve the angry reaction that came up inside him. He accepted my genuine feelings of compassion and received it as a healing balm for his wound. He felt comforted.

He acknowledged that his need for an apology and his angry belief that he'd never get one began in his childhood experiences and fueled his angry reaction.

I shared with him about my own childhood experiences around being wrongly accused and severely punished despite my innocence and how that fueled my defensiveness.

When we got through all the mess, we felt loved, understood, and resolved.

I still struggle. It's normal. Uncomfortable emotions are hard. Being brave enough to practice empathy with myself and with others makes the trek easier.

Brave Empathy

Creative – imaginative; generating original ideas; productive; innovative.

Inspired – aroused, influenced, or filled with a special feeling, thought, or motivation.

"Look at those pretty planets," Iris exclaimed with wonder. Her eyes widened as she saw the possibilities for fashioning her own universe. She squealed with delight as she spied a spaceship and astronaut on the shelf. Iris wondered how real spaceships travel from planet to planet. Deep in thought, Iris pondered, "What would it be like to travel in a spaceship or maybe, build one, or maybe she could build one and then travel in it? Where would she go? What would she see?" Iris laughed spontaneously at the thought. Iris felt creative and inspired.

Describe a time when you felt creative and inspired. What was it like for you?

Brave Empathy

Blocked – stopped or hindered by an obstacle.

Uninspired – lacking imagination, creativity or originality; without zest or enthusiasm.

Charlie wadded his paper up and threw it across the room. It landed next to the 3 other crumpled attempts. His head hurt, and his jaw ached from the tension in his muscles. He replayed the teacher's instructions on a constant loop in his head. He had no idea what she wanted from him. The assignment felt like a complete mystery as he sat and obsessed over the nightmare that was due the next day. He tried talking to himself, trying to generate some new ideas, but nothing came. He sighed miserably. He muttered to himself, "This is so stupid. I can't do this. I hate Mrs. Jennings. She's an idiot." Charlie felt blocked and uninspired.

When have you felt blocked or uninspired?

What helped you get past it?

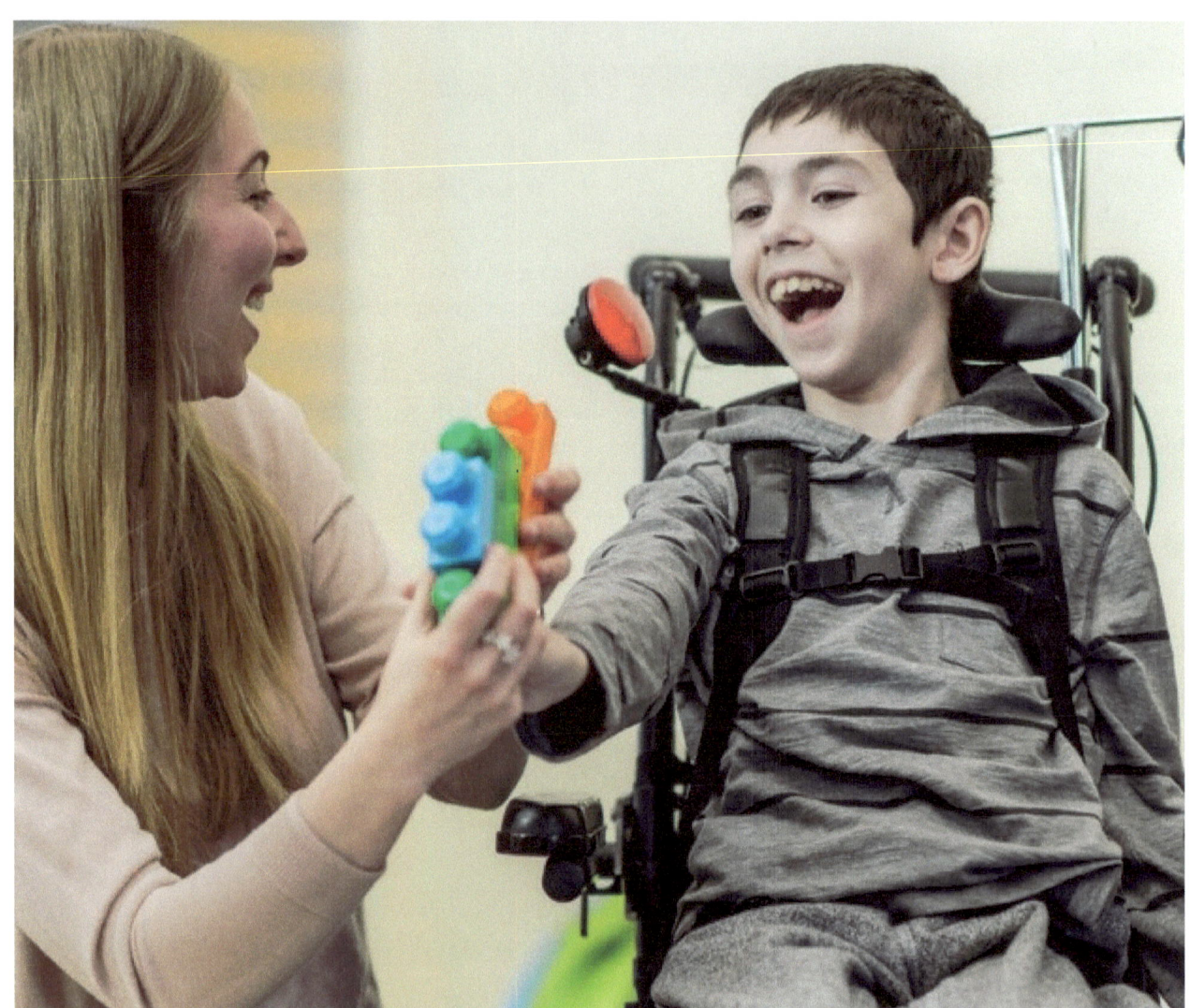

Connected – to have established successful communication and emotional exchange; to be actively engaged in a satisfying relationship; to be in harmony with another person.

Held – to feel faithfully cherished, treasured, and close; to feel steadfastly attached by the love, attention, and care of another.

Claire looked at her brother Hank with a smile that lit up her entire face. She gazed tenderly into Hank's eyes. Her heart swelled with joy. Claire wanted to savor the moments she shared with Hank. Claire knew she belonged when she was with Hank. She could tell he felt the warmth of their bond as keenly as she did when he laughed. Hank had a way of bringing out the best in Claire. Claire felt connected.

Hank looked forward to Claire's frequent visits. He knew he was important to her. He shoved at her playfully and grinned at her. He often told anyone he saw that his sister, Claire was going to come and visit him. He knew that since she had gone away to college, she liked to visit with him every chance she could. He noticed how her face brightened when she saw him. He knew that being with him made her happy. Hank felt held.

When have you felt connected or held?

Brave Empathy

Alone – feeling on one's own; separated from others; without aid, assistance, or help.

Lost – unable to find one's direction or way; ruined, crushed or destroyed; unable to understand or cope with a situation; beyond being found, recovered or salvaged.

Alena picked at her lunch. It all seemed so tasteless. She hadn't been sleeping well. Her first semester grades had been disastrous. She couldn't focus on her schoolwork. There were times when Alena couldn't get herself out of bed to go to classes. She kept thinking about how much she missed her family and friends back home. She'd been so eager about going away to college. She walked around campus not knowing where she was going wishing for the familiar sights of her old neighborhood. She never expected to feel so alone and lost.

Do you recall having felt alone and lost? Describe your experience.

Brave Empathy

Playful – full of energy and a desire for fun; good-natured and entertaining; lighthearted.

Jokey – eager to make people laugh; doing things in a way that is meant to be amusing, silly, or comical.

Jeff's face sparkled with a twinkle of mischief. He kept repeating, "Orange you glad I didn't say knock-knock! Jeff grabbed his sides as he bent over laughing uncontrollably. Jeff had just discovered knock-knock jokes. He repeated the joke to each of his friends and dissolved into laughter each time. It occurred to Jeff that he could make up his own versions of the joke. He fell to the ground and rolled around thinking about all the different things he could add to the joke to make it even funnier. Some of his ideas had him so tickled he nearly wet his pants. Jeff felt playful and jokey.

When did you feel playful and jokey?

Brave Empathy

Lifeless – lacking enthusiasm, strength, or excitement; someone who seems like he has no energy in him.

Burdened – carrying a heavy load; weighed down; bearing difficult, demanding responsibilities.

Blossom pressed her fingers into her temples. She had developed a headache. She kept wishing she could find a quiet spot to sit and be alone. She felt a little light-headed. She noticed she'd been snapping at her children the past few days. Blossom felt irritated with her husband, her mother, and her boss. It seemed everyone wanted something from her. She was exhausted. She leaned against the door frame. Blossom felt lifeless and burdened.

Have you ever felt lifeless or burdened?

What helped you to get your energy back?

Brave Empathy

Resilient – able to withstand or recover quickly from difficult situations; capable of withstanding shock without permanent damage; able to adjust to change easily.

Strong – able to withstand intense force or pressure; having or marked by abundant power; not easily injured, disturbed, subdued or taken.

Ricky appeared relaxed as he pulled himself up off the ground. He stretched and dusted himself off. Ricky bragged, "I'm strong. I can take it." He grabbed the rope and tried again to pull himself up. When he got to the top, he turned and smiled at his mom. "See, Mom. I'm really tough." Ricky felt resilient and strong.

When did you feel resilient?

When have you felt strong?

Brave Empathy

Uncompromising – to feel a reluctance or opposition to yield, compromise or make concessions to others; unwilling to change one's ways or opinions.

Decided – to feel that one has found a conclusion or solution; a dispute, doubt, or question feels settled; to feel a preference has been determined.

Daisy and her son, Doug, sat reviewing the questions Doug wanted to ask the Director of Student Disabilities while they waited for her to appear. Doug was prepared with his test results, and the psychologist's recommendation that he be given accommodations. "Mom, couldn't we just go home and forget about all this?" Doug asked Daisy.

Doug knew his rights and he knew the law. Daisy had made sure of that. Still, he felt ashamed of his learning disabilities and his need for accommodations. He wished he could play it cool and get by without any accommodations. He needed the accommodations but every time he thought about asking for them, he felt queasy. Every time he tried to back out of going to the meeting, Daisy had helped him strategize how to handle the obstacles he imagined he'd be facing.

Daisy and Doug had role-played as many possible scenarios as Doug and she could think of to prepare him for this meeting. Daisy was not going to let Doug's anxiety get in the way of his success in college. He was too smart to let that happen. Daisy acknowledged Doug's discomfort and stayed focused on their objective.

"You've got this, Doug. I believe in you. It makes sense you might be feeling a bit nervous right now. And, you're well prepared for this meeting. Focus on that." Daisy replied firmly. Doug felt encouraged by her words. Daisy felt decided and uncompromising.

When have you felt uncompromising or decided?

Brave Empathy

Chapter 5: Savor Comfortable Feelings

You've come half way in our journey together. Look at that view!

We've talked together about how complicated and changing feelings are. We've talked about how varied and valuable emotions are. We've looked at the definitions of emotions and empathy. We've looked at what it is to be brave. You've come a long way.

In the last 24 hours what feelings have you experienced? Were they intense and hard to ignore or mild and barely noticeable? How aware of your feelings are you on most days? Are you becoming more aware since starting this journey? Are the conversations you have in your head more likely to be about comfortable, pleasing things that have happened to you? Or are they about the uncomfortable things you experience? How much time do you spend talking to yourself and others about the comfortable things you think, feel, and experience as compared with the time you spend talking to yourself and others about the uncomfortable things you think, feel, and experience?

I read that most people have a bigger uncomfortable feeling word vocabulary than comfortable word vocabulary. That means we have fewer words to describe comfortable feelings. No wonder we're more likely to talk about uncomfortable things. The more you take the time to notice, think, write and talk about your positive, comfortable feelings, the more you'll be likely to think and feel those emotions in the future. This is because you're laying down new pathways for new thoughts in your brain.

The more you expand your conversations about these wonderful feelings, the more pathways you create in your brain for experiencing these new thoughts again and again. When you've got a big network of fantastic emotional experiences, one new experience will set off the memory of a whole bunch of other times you felt that feeling. Savoring your positive emotions helps you remember and re-experience them. Give it a try. It's like having a whole collection of souvenirs from your travels. It won't cost you a thing to store them besides the time it took to roll them over in your mind.

Go ahead. Give it a try. Think about a time when you felt happy recently. Where were you? Who were you with? What were you doing? What flavor of happy were you feeling? Choose some specific feeling words to describe your happy feelings. Does anything stand out about it?

Brave Empathy

Friendly – showing kindly interest, liking, and goodwill; like a friend, willing to help and support, ready and eager to be a friend.

Available – present or ready for immediate use; free, able willing to do something or to assume a responsibility.

"Daddy, would you like some tea?" Fran offered Alex, beaming politely as she began to pour the tea.

"Should I say it's good or yucky?" Alex asked cheerfully as he leaned in with his cup.

"Oh, Daddy, it's really nasty. You'll hate it," Fran replied trying to hold in her giggles. Alex screwed up his face and pretended to choke and cough out the make-believe disgusting liquid.

"Eew! This tea is hooor –ri –ble. I hate it," Alex exaggerated, as Fran shook with laughter. When she collected herself, she pretended to make a new pot of tea. This time she hummed and sang to herself as she worked.

"Have some more Dad. I promise it's good this time," Fran offered. She reached out again with the teapot smiling reassuringly. Fran and Alex feel friendly and available.

Describe a time when you felt friendly and available.

Brave Empathy

Mean – causing trouble or bother; displaying reactionary selfishness or cruelty; deliberately unkind.

Overloaded – to have too great a burden; having too much work, pressure, or responsibility.

Maris felt the sharp edges of the plastic press into her foot as she walked through her son Owen's bedroom. The pain shot up her foot and into her brain as she released a stream of curse words saved for just such occasions. The fact that she'd told him repeatedly to clean up his floor before he left for school flashed in her mind like a neon sign. All she could think was how much she wanted to grab up all the toys off his floor and toss them out the window. A string of unflattering names her dad had called her as a child when he was angry, rose up inside her. Without warning, she found herself attaching those names to Owen. Her mind was a whirl with the desire to strike out and hurt someone. The dog ran by and Maris cursed at him. She felt mean and angry.

Owen looked around his room. He slumped over his bed with his hands on his head. His step-brother's friends had made a huge mess of his room when he let them play in there over the weekend while he was away at his dad's house. He tried to be a good brother, but they had trashed his room big time. He knew his mom wanted him to clean it up before he went to school. There hadn't been enough time that weekend for him to get his homework done at dad's, study for the test he was having that morning at school and to clean his room when he got home from dad's. He knew that the room was important to his mom, but he also knew she wanted him to get good grades at school and turn in his homework on time. Owen remembered that Dad had told him to make sure he kept his grades up this quarter. Owen felt overloaded.

When have you felt mean? When have you felt overloaded?

Brave Empathy

Important – having power, authority, or influence; deserving or requiring more than ordinary attention, consideration or notice.

Valuable – worth a good price; having desirable or prized characteristics, traits, or qualities; of vast or significant use or service.

Vivian's face lit up with excitement. She pointed to her project and smiled with delight. After all her hard work, she'd won the competition. First prize. Her dad took her photo and posted it on Instagram and Facebook for the whole world to see. Her face beamed. She chattered away excitedly. "Can you believe it? First prize, Mom!" Vivian felt like she was floating a few inches off the ground. She felt important and valuable.

When have you felt important?

Write about a time when you felt valuable.

Brave Empathy

Useless – having no purpose, reason or good; not able to do what needs doing; ineffective.

Irrelevant – not important; not relating or connected to the matter at hand.

Ivan hung his head and kicked the leaves around absent-mindedly in his yard. His aunt had sent him outside to play. There was nothing he could do inside to help. The adults needed to talk. He'd just get in the way if he stayed. He didn't know what was up, but it seemed like it was a pretty big deal the way they were all looking so serious. They never seemed to need his opinion on things. After all, he was just a kid. "I probably couldn't do anything about it anyway. It's probably just some grown up stuff that doesn't have much to do with me," Ivan told himself. Still, he couldn't stop worrying about what was happening inside the house. Ivan felt useless and irrelevant.

I felt useless when …

The hardest thing about feeling irrelevant was …

Brave Empathy

Trusting – believing in someone or something; showing a desire to believe in someone's honesty or sincerity.

Trusted – regarded as honest and sincere; relied and depended on; a person one can go to for help, advice or information.

Tessa whispered her secret discovery into her mother, Trina's ear knowing that Momma would be happy for her and keep her secret. Tessa had just discovered that Daddy had bought Grandma a present and they were going to take it to her. Daddy had said it was a secret, but that she could share their secret with Momma. "Momma, I know you won't tell Grandma the secret. She's going to be so surprised when she sees us. Won't she be surprised, Momma? Tessa felt trusting.

Trina's face glowed with a smile that could warm all of Iceland on the coldest day of winter. She hugged Tessa close and listened carefully as Tessa whispered her secret into her ear. She celebrated the secret with her. "Oh, I won't tell a soul. Grandma will be so surprised." Trina felt trusted.

When was a time when you felt trusting? Who did you trust?

When was a time when you felt trusted? What was that like for you?

Brave Empathy

Uncertain – not completely confident or sure of someone or something; hesitant; having mixed feelings or conflicting ideas.

Misunderstood – having one's words or behavior taken wrongly or interpreted inaccurately.

Una stumbled along not sure of where to put her feet. She wasn't sure about the path Molly had chosen to take. It looked like it was going to be difficult to get over, around, and through. There certainly wasn't a clear trail to follow. "Whose idea was it to come this way? Una asked Molly. Una reached her hand out for Molly's as she decided whether she would take another step forward or try to turn and go back. Una felt uncertain.

Molly smiled at Una and took her hand. She suspected that when she'd invited Una along that Una hadn't really understood the challenges she'd be facing on the journey. She'd tried to prepare her but until a person had hiked this way it was difficult to imagine what it was really like. Molly recalled that each time she took this trip, it was a little different and unpredictable. It was impossible to fully prepare someone for an adventure like this one. Molly felt confident that Una could do it.

Molly knew from experience that they were closer to their destination than they were to their starting point and she could see that Una was doing her best and feeling hesitant. She knew that Una trusted her, and she could see that trust wavering. Molly felt misunderstood. She was confident that she and Una would arrive safely at their destination. "It's okay Una. We'll be there within the next half hour. It's just through here. This is the hardest part. I promise."

Can you recall a time when you felt uncertain? When did you feel misunderstood?

Brave Empathy

Chapter 6: Sympathy

Compassion moves us to want to help.

Empathy is being aware my son, Ryan, is having a feeling and then, naming that feeling. I notice the look on his face, the way he knocked over the lamp, and I hear the words coming out of his mouth, "I hate school. I'm not going to that school ever again. They're all stupid!" I recognize that he's having a strong and uncomfortable emotion. I believe what he is feeling is frustrated.

Compassion is the feeling I experience that makes me want to do something to help my child manage the emotion I noticed he's having.

I guess that Ryan's frustrated. It's an educated guess. I feel compassion for him, and I want to do something to help him with that frustration. It would be natural to want to take away his frustration, so he'd feel better. It's hard to see him that frustrated. I want to go to school and make them change the way they do things so that he will be successful. He wants to do well at school. With his learning challenges, it's harder for him. I want to force them to help him. I get caught up in my own feelings of fear and frustration.

School was where I learned to believe in myself. School was where I learned that I mattered. I want my son to have the same good experience I had growing up. I feel frustrated that I can't make the people at his school understand what he needs, what I need.

The situation is unfair and just plain wrong. I feel sorry for my son and for myself. It doesn't take long before I'm spiraling down into my own thoughts, feelings, and story. I've created a whole bunch of thoughts in my own head after seeing my son's frustration. I find myself caught up in these overwhelming thoughts and feelings. Feeling sorry for Ryan, feeling sorry for myself, has taken me down a dead-end path. I've missed what's happening with him. I stopped listening. I got caught in a downward spiral of sympathy. Did you know, when people are hurting, they rarely want our pity or sympathy?

The definition of sympathy that I found most helpful to understand it's troubling nature is "an unwanted, pity-based response to a distressing situation, characterized by a lack of understanding and self-preservation."

Brave Empathy

Hurting people don't want our sympathy.

What people want when they're hurting is empathy and compassion. They welcome our genuine desire to help ease their discomfort once they see we're interested in understanding their feelings and circumstances. Our empathy and compassion ease their hopelessness and isolation. Our gift of empathy helps people feel seen, heard, and understood. Our compassion moves us to find a way of helping that meets their need.

When I stopped listening to my son, I got lost in myself. I wasn't available to meet Ryan's need because I was too busy figuring out for myself what I thought he needed, what I thought I needed, and not listening to what he needed. I was motivated to ease my own discomfort. Happily, I realized all that before I got trapped in a blind alley.

Here's what I know. Empathy comes before learning. Without empathy, we leave our kids in an emotionally charged state where they can't process what we're saying to them. They can't listen.

Empathy meets their emotional needs and brings them back to a state of calm, turning back on their thinking brain, calming the emotion center in their brain and preparing them to listen and remember. I knew I needed to know more about what Ryan was thinking and feeling. I needed him to tell me more.

By bringing myself back to focusing on Ryan, instead of myself, I was able to tune into what he was saying. When he felt understood, his emotions shifted. Then, he felt guilty and ashamed of how he had behaved. He laid on the couch and cried out the overwhelming emotions that washed over him. I kept listening, focusing on bravely identifying what he was feeling and staying compassionate. I could see that he was struggling with these painful and uncomfortable feelings. It worked.

My compassion and empathy helped him get through the moment until he bounced back. Soon, he was ready to pick himself up and get on with the day. We decided what he needed was a break before he started his homework that afternoon. He helped reset the lamp and straighten the mess he made before running off to play for a while. Later, he settled down to his homework refreshed and ready to work. When I was reacting to Ryan with sympathy and pity, I disconnected from him. When I returned to empathy, I reconnected.

He didn't want me to go down to his school and fix things for him. He wanted me to see how overwhelmed and frustrated he was right then. He needed my loving connection.

Once I saw that, we were able to work together to figure out he needed some time to recover from the stress he was feeling before tackling the homework his teacher had assigned him for that day.

Once he got his need for understanding and caring met, he was ready to engage in problem solving with me. His thinking brain was able to re-engage. Feeling close and connected, we teamed up to solve the problem together. We didn't spend more than twenty minutes that day, but my son learned an important lesson about the power of empathy that he hasn't forgotten as an adult.

When Ryan talks about his work, I hear him expressing empathy for his co-workers. I hear him expressing empathy for his wife. I hear him expressing empathy towards his father. When he tells me about the things happening in his life, I know that my investment was worth every ounce of bravery and effort I put into listening. My resolve to keep listening with empathy is strengthened.

Come visit me at www.facebook.com/playconnect and tell me more about a challenge you've had since starting this journey with me. Share a triumph you've experienced along the way. Tell me about you.

Brave Empathy

Energetic – having the strength and enthusiasm required for continued physical or mental activity.

Free – able to be, do, have, or feel as one wishes; not subject to the control or commands of another; released from restraints and restrictions.

Emma and her daughter, Farryn danced to their favorite song as the wind blew gently around them. They swayed their bodies to the beat of the music. The lyrics flowed through the trees and caressed the countryside with joy. Emma felt full of energy as she watched Farryn swing her arms freely in the air over her head. Emma imitated her daughter's moves mirroring her movements. Emma felt energetic.

Farryn loved seeing her Mommy dance with her. She loved the way the wind played in her hair as she moved. She moved her arms and bounced her legs in time with the music. She spun around and fell down laughing. "You try it, Mommy!" Farryn giggled as she got up and spun around again. Farryn felt free.

Write about a time when you felt free and energetic.

Brave Empathy

Exhausted – drained of one's physical or mental resources; completely used up; depleted of energy, stamina, or strength.

Trapped – to feel unable to move or be freed; restrained; unable to escape an unpleasant situation.

Ellen put on her favorite pair of shoes, a pretty spring dress, and went outside. It was too beautiful a day to stay cooped up inside. She was tired of washing dishes and cleaning house. She deserved a break. She laid down in the car with her feet out the window and soaked in the healing energy from the sun. She realized that she had used up the last of her energy. "This is just what I needed," Ellen told herself. "I just can't go back into that house and face the rest of the cleaning until I get some change of perspective. It's impossible to keep that house clean. I don't know what I'm going to do if they don't learn to pick up after themselves. It's a never-ending battle." Ellen felt exhausted and trapped.

When have you felt exhausted?

When did you feel trapped? What did you do about it?

Brave Empathy

Happy – feeling or showing pleasure or contentment; enjoying a condition or situation.

Lighthearted – free from care, anxiety or worry; untroubled; cheerful.

Harrison stretched his arms wide into the air and smiled at his mom. "Mom, I'm going to buy you a castle in Scotland. You're going to love it." His voice was light and bubbly. He moved his arms fluidly through the air as he spoke. The wind blew through his curls. The sun lit his face. "Mom, I want to buy flowers for you to wear in your hair. I think you'd look pretty with flowers in your hair. I think you're the most beautiful mom in the whole wide world." Harrison leaned against his mom and smiled up at her. Harrison was feeling happy and lighthearted.

When have you felt happy and lighthearted?

How did you express those feelings?

Brave Empathy

Sad – feeling or showing sorrow, grief, or unhappiness; related to feelings of loss, despair, or disappointment.

Sorry – feeling sorrowful regret; sad or distressed because of sympathy with someone else's misfortune.

Shelby sat alone in his room as looked out the window. His eyes glazed over as if he really wasn't looking at anything special. He'd long ceased to care what was beyond the window. He bent forward and laid his forehead on the glass. His movement lacked energy. In his hand was the note from his girlfriend, Susan, breaking off their relationship. Even though it had been a couple of weeks since she left the note in his locker at school, Shelby felt sad.

Susan avoided Shelby's phone calls and text messages. She didn't know what to say to him since she'd broken off their relationship. Things with him had gotten too intense too fast and her parents thought she should focus on getting ready to go to college instead of worrying about a boyfriend. She had tried to reason with Shelby, but he didn't seem to understand how important it was to her to get into a good college. She tried to apologize to him but nothing Susan said seemed to help. Susan reached for her phone to try and compose another text message to Shelby. She didn't want to get back together. She just didn't want Shelby to feel so sad. Susan felt sorry.

I felt sad when …

I felt sorry when …

Chapter 7: Kids and Empathy

Kids imagine what it's like to be mom when they play house, pretending to change baby's diaper and cooking dinner. When kids dress up like a fireman and put out imaginary fires, they take the perspective of the fireman rushing to save the day. When a little girl puts on a toy stethoscope and listens to my heart, she's imagining what it's like to be the doctor she saw last week.

As kids play, they take on the perspective of others in their world. They're doing the work of empathy. Imagining what it might be like to be someone else is an important part of developing empathy. Kids gain perspective-taking experience in play. When a girl changes a doll's diaper, looks at me with a disgusted look on her face, and tells me that the diaper stinks, she imagines how mom feels changing her little brother's diaper. She feels disgust pretending to change the diaper. She imagines that mom feels disgusted changing diapers.

When she picks that doll up and cuddles it in her arms and talks soothingly to it, she's imagining a mom feeling love for her baby. The act of pretending awakens feelings of love in her. She puts her own love into the work of pretending. She imagines mom feels loving when mom soothes baby brother. She's discovering what it is like to be a loving mother.

When kids pretend, things in their world begin to make sense, things that before didn't make sense.

Playing at feeling disgust helps kids recognize when they see someone feeling disgust. They experience feeling disgust as they play out things they associate with disgusting. It might be things they've felt disgusted by or it might be things others have shown disgust towards. I'll spare you a detailed description of the stuff kids play while they're figuring out disgust, contempt, and disapproval. If you're a parent, you've seen enough bodily function type play to know what I'm talking about. When kids play these things out, they're creating an understanding about disgust.

Most of the time, when kids play, they don't have someone naming the feeling, so the emotional experience isn't organized into a clearly identified category with a name attached. As a result, when you ask your child what he's feeling, he can't tell you. He doesn't know. He hasn't described the experience to himself with words that he then stored into his long-term memory, so he doesn't have the words to tell you about what he felt. Having someone notice and name the feeling while the play is happening is a powerful way to build empathy and a feeling word vocabulary.

When a parent or child counselor notices and names the feelings, a child is spontaneously playing out, the child pairs the feelings with the feeling word that names the emotion. The combination of words and experience builds the structures in the brain for understanding and organizing emotions with language in the brain. This pairing of play with feeling words is different than giving a child a worksheet with feeling faces and words to memorize.

The memorized information is stored in the learning and memory center of the brain which is temporarily shut down when a child gets into a highly charged emotional state like anger. Because of that, a child who is furious is not going to have access to the information he memorized from a worksheet about what to do when he's mad. Because the learning and memory center of his brain is temporarily and involuntarily turned off, a terrified child doesn't have access to the information he learned in a book about what to do when he's feeling afraid. He simply can't access material he's learned in this way.

If he's had the experience of having this feeling noticed and named as scared and terrified over and over in play, he's developed the pairing of the emotional experience with the name of the feeling in his brain and has widely developed his own personal experience of what scared and terrified is. He may even be able to say to his mom, "Mom, I feel really scared right now." He has the words and the experience to notice and identify his own feelings.

Noticing and naming a child's feelings in play creates a rich and full network in her brain and body for understanding the emotions she feels throughout the day.

As humans we're bombarded with comfortable and uncomfortable feelings every day. When we notice, recognize and can readily name those feelings, in ourselves first and then, in others around us, we are ready to mention and manage feelings effectively and respectfully. The brain hates uncertainty and works to fill in gaps in information. The things our emotionally charged brain constructs to fill in the gap when we don't have all the information to explain something, is faulty at best.

The more familiar we are with our emotional experiences the easier it is to mention and manage our feelings and the faulty explanations we created to manage our discomfort with not knowing. Brené Brown refers to the story created by this tendency to rush to fill the gap as the Stormy First Draft. When kids play and we notice and name their feelings, we're helping kids to unravel the tangle of stormy first drafts they have created about themselves, others, and the way the world works.

When I first saw this approach to noticing and naming children's feelings, it didn't seem like a big deal. Yet, the evidence was overwhelming. The mountain of studies comparing the results all said the same thing. This way of noticing and naming kids' feelings empowers kids to mention and manage their feelings, equips them with great people skills, and enables them to bounce back from stress.

I've seen kids bounce back from the normal overwhelming day to day stress we're all experiencing, and I've seen kids bounce back from unspeakable, traumatizing things, that most of us hope we never experience.

This noticing and naming feelings skill is one part of a whole set of skills I use in play therapy. Watching it done, you wouldn't think there was anything so special about it.

While I'm not advocating noticing and naming every feeling your child has all day, every day, I am saying that used in the context of a 30-minute, once a week, playtime with your child, it builds an incredible foundation for a lifetime of empathy and emotional fluency.

I can't fully teach you all the trade secrets I use in these weekly play-times here because that would fill up too many pages. I can give you some suggestions for using this noticing and naming feelings skill at home with your own child.

When your child is playing, and shows you a drawing he's made, notice the look on his face and the sound of his voice. A smile on his face and the way he's shaking his picture in your face, might indicate that he's feeling proud and excited to show you his work. Responding with a smile as you take the picture to look at it, you can add, "You look so proud and excited to show me your picture." Delight with your child in his feeling of pride and excitement. The repetition of this simple process as you notice and name your child's feelings during relaxed and comfortable interactions with him sets up a pattern for his being able to notice and name his own comfortable feelings.

It doesn't have to be every time. It doesn't even have to be once every day. I do this for kids in once a week play therapy sessions. Over a matter of weeks, parents and teachers notice a change in the way kids mention and manage their emotions. With repetition, the experience of having one's feelings noticed and named stacks up to build a rich and varied feeling word vocabulary anchored in personal experience. Try it. Notice and name what you're feeling.

Engaged – greatly interested; to feel intensely involved, absorbed, or engrossed; committed.

Determined – being set on a decision; firmly resolved not to change; displaying a strong desire to stick to a certain plan of action even if it is difficult.

Eddie sat on the edge of his chair and leaned forward as he pressed the screwdriver into the plastic wheel. He turned it as he focused his gaze intently. He had his hammer ready in his other hand. "You're working so hard on that," his grandpa commented. Eddie continued his work without breaking his concentration to answer. After a while, Eddie turned to his grandpa and said excitedly, "This truck is like yours, Grandpa." Then he turned his attention to another wheel. Eddie felt engaged and determined.

When have you felt engaged?

When did you feel determined?

Brave Empathy

Indifferent – having no significant interest or sympathy; unconcerned; having no special liking for or dislike of something.

Unsettled – not decided or determined; not answered or worked out; uncertain; to feel or show doubt, indecision.

Isaac walked through the mall beside his mom at a slow, steady pace. His arms hung limply at his sides. He looked sleepy. He really didn't want to come shopping. He could think of a hundred other things he'd rather be doing. When his mom asked him if he liked something, he shrugged reluctantly. She offered to get him something to eat. "No," he replied in a flat voice, smiling with a polite but false smile. Isaac felt indifferent.

Isaac's mom, Uma wanted to buy Isaac a birthday present, but he was not cooperating. She bit her lip and frowned. She glanced at Isaac to see if she could read what he was thinking. When she couldn't read him, she asked his opinion. Uma tilted her head from side to side, weighing her choices. Uma felt unsettled.

When have you felt indifferent?

When did you feel unsettled?

Brave Empathy

Overjoyed – feeling great pleasure or delight; deeply pleased and happy.

Eager – wanting to do or have something very much; enthusiastic willingness; impatient desire.

Olive bounced on her toes. She talked over her dad, Oren, when he tried to ask her what she thought. "Daddy, this is the best!" Her eyes were wide as she looked at view of the ocean. She fired a series of questions at her dad as she ran up and down the beach. She blew out a long breath and smiled. She looked her dad in the eye and asked, "Have you ever seen anything so beautiful, Dad?" Olive felt eager and overjoyed.

Oren laughed with delight to see Olive's eager excitement. His eyes danced. He gave Olive an enthusiastic thumbs up. He swung his arms as he tried to keep up with Olive. He held his arms out wide wishing he could hug the whole world. Oren had been planning this trip to the ocean for months and he couldn't be happier with Olive's response. Oren felt overjoyed.

When have you felt overjoyed?

When have you felt eager?

Brave Empathy

Devastated – shattered or distraught; brought to a state of ruin or destruction; to feel destroyed completely.

Reluctant – unwilling, hesitant and showing doubt; not wanting to do, be, have, or feel something.

Darren clutched his stuffed bear and wailed. He tugged at his hair and rocked himself. He clenched his jaw and turned his head to the wall. "I want my puppy," he sobbed. Darren, age 5, wasn't taking the loss of the family pet well. Darren felt devastated.

Ruby, Darren's mom, swallowed hard and pressed her lips together. She looked pained. Ruby mulled over the idea of getting a new dog for the family, but she wasn't sure what would be best for Darren. Darren's dad, Douglas, thought they needed a new dog as soon as possible. "Maybe," Ruby answered. She got up and walked across the room. "I need more time to think about it," she added as she left the room. Ruby felt reluctant.

When have you felt devastated?

When have you felt reluctant?

Brave Empathy

Innocent – feeling pure; lacking an awareness of evil; free from guilt, blame or fault; free from malicious or immoral influence.

Virtuous – feeling a sense of integrity and high moral standards; ethical; feeling commendable qualities such as honesty, decency, and honor; doing the right thing.

Ivory skipped through the grass. She ran up to her sister Violet and hugged her. "Oh Violet, I can't believe how kind you are. Thank you for playing with me. I just love these bubbles. It feels like the whole world is perfect. I don't want this to ever end. I could stay here with you forever. Wouldn't it be great if everyone could lay here in the grass and blow bubbles together? We'd all have such fun." Ivory felt innocent.

Violet hugged her sister, Ivory, and thanked her for her sweet words. "I don't think we can stay here forever but it is nice to think about this pleasant feeling lasting forever." Violet looked thoughtful as she continued, "I'm so glad I decided to bring you out here today. I thought you'd love it. I know how much you enjoy getting outside and how cooped up you get when you're stuck inside all day," Violet added. Violet would have been content staying home and reading her book, but she knew that Ivory needed some adventure. Violet felt virtuous.

When have you felt innocent?

When have you felt virtuous?

Brave Empathy

Guilty – responsible for a wrongdoing, fault or error; feeling uncomfortable because of a belief that you have done something bad or wrong.

Monstrous – to feel extraordinarily hideous, vicious, disgusting, abnormal or wrong.

Gene's stomach felt like he might vomit. His chest felt like there was an elephant sitting on it. There was a pain in the back of his throat. He kept replaying the incident in his mind. If only he could go back and change things. If only there was someone, anyone, he could talk to about what he'd done. He knew what he'd said was wrong. If only there was a way to make it right. Gene felt guilty.

Gene pulled at his collar and tried to lighten the mood with a joke. He hoped he could distract his family from remembering what he'd said to his grandmother. He wanted to run away but that would be too obvious. "How could I have been so awful? What kind of idiot am I?" he wondered. Gene was convinced he deserved a severe tongue lashing. "I was wrong to even open my mouth. I should have kept quiet. I always get in trouble when I try to stand up for myself. Gene felt monstrous.

When was a time when you felt guilty?

Have you felt monstrous? What happened?

Brave Empathy

Chapter 8: Adjust Uncomfortable Feelings

How do I want to feel as I live my life? It's a good question to ask myself. What feeling would I like to invite more of into my life? How can I invite more comfortable feelings into my life? What do I do with all those uncomfortable feelings that come in uninvited?

I am not my emotion. My emotion is a part of me, but it is not all of me. I'm more than my feelings. There's my will, the part of me that makes decisions about who I choose to be and what I choose to do and what I make of my experiences. I have my experiences that shape and influence how I see myself, others, and the world. I'm influenced by the people in my life, my relationships, both comfortable and uncomfortable ones.

I am complex and amazing.

You are too.

I imagine you're like me. You have times when you feel overwhelmed, times when your feelings decide your actions. Most of us have times when we regret the things we did or said and wish we had kept those emotions in check.

Emotions function like a compass sending us information about when to move ahead and when to duck for cover. Unfortunately, as a compass our emotions are far from perfect. It's easy for our emotions to take us in the wrong direction. We may even find ourselves approaching and avoiding the wrong people and situations.

It's normal to get off track sometimes. Discovering how and when to trust our emotional compass is key to knowing how to operate a human body and mind, equipped with a standard set of complicated feelings. Our emotions have remarkable potential for helping us navigate the world when we know how to use them skillfully.

While we don't have complete control, we do have a lot more influence over our feelings than you might think. What's more interesting is that the people who study the science of emotions have discovered that when we believe we have some control over our emotions, we're more likely to effectively use strategies to change our emotions.

Brave Empathy

What if we anchored ourselves in the firm belief that we can alter our emotions when we need to?

The processes we use to influence and adjust our emotions are known as emotional regulation. Maybe you've cheered yourself up by doing something you like to do. Maybe you've made yourself anxious by dwelling on a worrisome thought for too long. If you've done either of these two things, you've changed your emotions.

Here's another example of regulating one's emotions. You're having an argument with your spouse and you decide to take an urgent call from a client. You know you need to pull yourself together for the call. You change your tone of voice, facial expression and by the end of the conversation you discover your emotions have changed. You find yourself thinking differently about the argument. You regulated your emotions in order to have the conversation with your client.

No matter how happy or well-adjusted we are, we'll also have feelings we'd rather not have. Uncomfortable feelings aren't automatically bad, or feelings that should never be felt. Accepting that uncomfortable feelings are a normal part of life makes them less distressing. Believing we can tolerate the discomfort while it lasts and knowing it will pass because emotions are temporary, helps us maintain our perspective.

Having a feeling doesn't mean that I am required to act. Acting on a feeling can intensify and prolong an emotion. That could be a good thing if you want to extend and strengthen a comfortable feeling.

However, if it's an uncomfortable feeling, I may need to pause before deciding what course of action I want to take. Typically, when I'm experiencing an intensely uncomfortable feeling, the thinking part of my brain isn't functioning at its best. Pausing gives my thinking brain an opportunity to catch up with my emotions.

I don't recommend venting feelings by ranting and shouting, nor do I recommend trying to not think about unpleasant things. Attempts to vent feelings through ranting intensifies and prolongs the uncomfortable feelings.

Avoidance sends the feelings underground where they fester and grow. Although these things may provide temporary relief, these strategies risk making things worse in the long run.

Smiling when I'm angry to disguise my emotions is not regulating my angry feelings. Suppressing the expression of an emotion is different than regulating or adjusting the emotion itself.

Focus on increasing your comfortable feelings. Write them down. Savor the details that brought about the comfortable feelings. Turn them over in your mind. Re-experience them in your memory. Actively work to cement them in your long-term memory.

Extend and intensify them by talking about these feelings with others, reminiscing, and re-creating the events that brought about these feelings whenever possible. Use these strategies to put more comfortable feelings into your life. It's said that happy people average about three comfortable feelings to every one uncomfortable feeling they experience. When you notice uncomfortable feelings are increasing beyond that, be sure to schedule some pleasant activities into your day.

I'm not saying ignore your uncomfortable feelings, I'm saying make sure to create enough comfortable ones to provide an average of about three to one whenever you can.

There are strategies you can use to reduce the intensity of an uncomfortable emotion. Pausing before you act is a start. Noticing and naming your feeling is a good next step. Refusing to engage in or get stuck on thoughts and behaviors that intensify and prolong the uncomfortable feelings is another step in the right direction.

Connecting with a supportive friend, not venting or ranting, not trying to get them on your side against someone else, but rather telling your friend about the feeling you noticed and named and about what you think may have brought on the feeling without blaming others or making them the villain in your stormy first draft can help.
Exploring the role, you think you played, in the situation that led to the uncomfortable feeling can help you find a new perspective or solution.

I find that after 30 minutes of brushing, scraping, and smearing acrylic paint colors on canvas, not worrying about what it looks like, my emotions change. My thinking brain comes back online and the rage and frustration that drove me to seek solace in my art room settles. Hope emerges. My perspective shifts enough that I can think about the thing that sparked my emotion more clearly. I find my brave empathy and compassion. I see possibilities to solve the problem that didn't occur to me earlier.

Brave Empathy

Doing something you enjoy doing can change your emotions.

Kids experience this when they play out their frustrations and rage. Play reduces stress and helps kids bounce back. Particularly when a supportive adult is present and accepting without judging. Kids play out their uncomfortable feelings and try out solutions in imaginative play. In the process their emotions change. Their thinking brains are turned back on. They see things from a new perspective.

There are a lot of other strategies, but these will get you through many of the uncomfortable feelings most of us experience.

There are times when our uncomfortable feelings require the help of a professional counselor. Clients who come to my office for counseling find caring confidential support when they need something beyond what friends can give or when they need additional strategies for getting through uncomfortable, painful or stuck feelings.

For parents, managing your own feelings comes before being able to help your child regulate his. It's a lot like putting the oxygen mask on yourself on the airplane before trying to get your child's oxygen mask on him. You can't help your child with his mask, if you pass out from lack of oxygen first.

Children have a more difficult time regulating their feelings because the parts of their brains that handle impulse control and strategic thinking are not fully developed. Because the human brain takes about twenty-five years to fully develop, our expectations about their behavior is sometimes not in line with their ability to behave in ways we consider socially appropriate. A human brain develops from the back to the front, meaning that kids have a greater capacity to feel emotion than they do to describe it with words or to plan and produce well thought out behavior, particularly when they're feeling an intense emotion.

Kids are better at spontaneously creating stories in play that represent some aspect of what they're feeling. For this reason, play therapists have successfully used play to help kids regulate and adjust their uncomfortable feelings for the last fifty years. Brave empathy, noticing and naming a child's feelings while he plays, is one of the most important skills I use in the playroom. I give kids a name to associate with those uncomfortable things churning inside and coming out as bad behavior.

Surprisingly, once I name a child's feelings with care and concern, she feels understood.

The respectful caring response is enough to meet her needs. 7 times out of 10, nothing more is needed. The problem ends there. The child moves on to more satisfying pursuits. With repetition, kids pair their feelings with the words that name emotions and eventually, noticing and naming feelings becomes natural.

When kids can't self-regulate those uncomfortable feelings come out as behavior. Some scream if they don't get their way. Others lash out with their fists. Some bully. Some withdraw. Others become anxious or depressed. They have problems with teachers and classmates. They get excluded, teased and harassed by other kids. Unfortunately, behavior problems eventually, influence grades. Other kids hold it together for as long as they can and meltdown at home.

Children who can regulate their emotions return to calm more quickly after an upset. They don't need mom to calm them as often. Moms spend less time soothing upset children so that they have more time to snuggle with happy children. They whine less. They don't need to act out to get what they want. They get along better with other kids. They're more well-liked by their classmates and by their teachers. They do better in school because they're able to focus their attention.

Kids who easily bounce back are more popular with their peers. This helps them make friends and keep the friends they have. Kids who can recognize and understand feelings navigate and resolve conflicts. Kids who can't, grow into adults who can't manage relationship conflicts.

When parents regulate their own emotions, they set the example for their kids. Then, when parents respond to their child's behavior and emotions with brave empathy, it helps regulate their children's emotions. As a result of experience and modeling, kids develop empathy and emotional regulation. Your commitment to practice brave empathy will equip you to build emotional regulation in yourself, and in your children. Did you realize when we started this trip that noticing and naming feelings from time to time could have such a powerful impact on so many?

When you need to turn down the temperature of an uncomfortable feeling you're experiencing, try flipping through this book and looking at the photos. I chose pictures that I think you'll find comforting to your system. You've discovered so many good things on this journey. Stay with me. We're getting close to the end but there's more good stuff ahead. You won't want to miss this next part.

Helpful – to make it easier for someone to do a job or deal with a problem; to give assistance or aid; to ease or lighten someone's burden.

Prepared – ready in body and mind to be used for some purpose or activity; trained and equipped.

Hayley smiled at her mom as she put the lettuce into the grocery cart. "I'm a good shopper, Mom." "You know just how to pick out the lettuce," her mom replied. "You like helping me shop." Hayley's face glowed with pride. She walked with a bounce in her step looking around to see where the carrots were. "I'll get the carrots, Mom." Hayley felt helpful.

Hayley's sister, Penelope, returned with the eggplant her mom had asked her to go get. Penelope gave her mom and Hayley an easy nod as she approached the cart. She looked calm, relaxed, and at ease. "I got the best one there, just like you showed me, Mom," Penelope said to her mom. "Thanks for showing me how to pick those out last time." "What did you get, Hayley?" she asked her sister in a friendly voice. Penelope felt prepared.

When have you felt helpful?

When have you felt prepared?

Disruptive – stopping something from continuing as usual by causing disturbance, interruption, or distraction; characterized by unrest or turmoil; troubling one's peace of mind; challenging the status quo.

Surprised – shocked or amazed by something unexpected; struck with wonder and astonishment at something out of the ordinary.

Dillan unbuttoned the top button of his shirt and pulled at his collar. He shifted his weight wishing he could leave. He cleared his throat. Dillan wondered how much longer he'd be able to take his dad's bragging about his sister's good grades. Again. Today of all days. All he could think about was the big math test he had to take this morning. He knew Dad was going to be disappointed if he failed that test. "All you care about is grades!" Dillan shouted suddenly at his Dad. He wished his dad would talk about something else. He bolted from the table, spilling a glass of orange juice he'd left half full next to his breakfast plate. Dillan felt disruptive.

A surge of adrenaline shot through Shae's body. She gasped as the glass crashed onto the floor, breaking into pieces. She tightened her grip on her glass and pulled her plate closer to her as if to keep it safe from the mess spilling around her. "What's that about?" she asked her dad. Shae felt surprised.

Have you felt disruptive? What happened?

When have you felt surprised?

Brave Empathy

Powerful – having great strength, authority, prestige, or influence; having a strong impact on someone or something.

Heroic – a feeling that motivates courageous, daring, noble, or self-sacrificing action; willing to take extreme measures for the good of others.

Poppy aimed her sword with an alert gaze. Her feet were planted firmly into the ground. Her shoulders pushed back. She looked calm and focused as she sized up her imaginary opponent. She looked him right in the eye and asked, "Are you ready to pay for your crimes, You Miserable Tyrant?" She laughed with confidence and added, "I will make you pay! You'll be sorry you ever messed with me and my family." Poppy smiled a playful grin, certain the villain would soon be defeated. Poppy felt powerful and heroic.

I felt powerful when …

I felt heroic when …

Brave Empathy

Weak – likely to fail under pressure, stress, or strain; lacking physical strength, energy, persuasiveness, skill, or authority; lacking essential elements, or qualities needed to do a thing.

Sidelined – out of action; incapable of playing in the game; to be in an unavailable, unusable condition; removed to a less important job, rank, or level; made to observe rather than participate in an activity.

Wyatt's throat was dry. He couldn't seem to focus on what his friends were saying to him. They were all thrilled about the talent show but he couldn't quite get excited about it. The idea of getting out on that stage in front of the whole school made him feel queasy. "I don't know guys. Couldn't we skip this one? I don't think this crowd is ready for my talents," Wyatt quipped trying to cover his discomfort. "You'll be fine, Man," his friend Sid replied. You can watch from back stage and make sure all our props are all ready when we need them. Nobody'll see you." Wyatt felt weak and sidelined.

When have you felt weak?

When did you feel sidelined?

Brave Empathy

Congratulations! You made it to through all 80 feelings, the comfortable ones and the uncomfortable ones. Did you know there were so many different feelings a person could feel? And I didn't even include every possible feeling word. There's so many I didn't include because I didn't want to overwhelm you.

I hope you'll keep discovering new feeling words to include in your own feeling word vocabulary. Exploring feelings is a lifelong journey. You're off to a great start. You discovered a whole lot of things about empathy, and bravery, and emotional regulation and about how feelings work.

You discovered that an emotion is a natural reaction to something that happens, combined with our thoughts about the thing that happened, experienced as sensations in the body that influence behavior. You saw that empathy is being aware of and able to accurately identify the feelings of another. You discovered that you can choose to notice and accept someone's uncomfortable feeling, without rushing to change it and bravely tolerate your own discomfort while noticing and naming the feeling. You found that the processes we use to influence and adjust our emotions are known as emotional regulation.

You discovered that emotions come and go and are temporary. You discovered that believing you can adjust your feelings, up and down, is key to being able to bring more comfortable feelings into your life and using your uncomfortable feelings as information. You discovered that feelings can serve as a compass and have a valuable purpose. You discovered that anger motivates a person to do what needs to be done to correct an injustice and joy shows us what to do more of.

You discovered that suppressing the anger with a smile isn't the same as adjusting your anger. Naming and noticing that you're angry and considering what you're angry about, exploring the stormy first draft story you're telling yourself, and what you need to feel resolved are all important steps in using your uncomfortable feelings well. You discovered that ignoring your feelings doesn't work to change them.

You discovered that helping kids with their emotions begins with noticing and naming your own feelings. You discovered that kids develop empathy and the ability to mention and manage emotions instead of acting out when we notice and name their feelings. You discovered that kids need help with their emotions because their emotions develop before their ability to put their feelings into words. Along the way we looked at what happens when kids can't mention and manage their emotions.

We saw that they whine, and act out, and even withdraw. You discovered that even adults have difficulties mentioning and managing the behavior sparked by emotions.

You're well equipped to begin noticing and naming feelings you see in the world around you. Even with all you've discovered so far, there's still a lot more to see and discover in the realm of emotions. There's so much more to experience for yourself. I've given you a couple of pages to record additional feeling words you want to add to your collection. I hope you'll feel exuberated as you explore the wide world of emotions. Make a list of comfortable feelings you've yet to experience and start planning how to bring them into your life.

As we're nearing the place where we're saying goodbye, I'm aware of all the things I haven't yet shared with you. There's so much more I'd love to tell you about empathy and feelings that I've discovered in my travels. I don't want our time together to end here.

How about instead of saying goodbye, we make it see you later? Come on over to my Facebook group, Play Connect Influence and tell me about a joyful experience you're planning. You'll find the group at: https://www.facebook.com/groups/playconnect/

I hope we can continue the conversation about emotions, empathy, the kids, and the delights of parenthood. If we were having this conversation at your favorite coffee shop, we'd be talking about many things. Things like your feelings about being a parent, the feelings you see your kids struggling with, the ways you want them to feel.

Hey, let's continue the conversation over in my Facebook group, Play Connect Influence. Stop in and let me know if you prefer coffee or tea. Milk and sugar? A breakfast sandwich or a sweet pastry?

You'll find more goodies for you over in the group. I'll be sharing more thoughts and helpful tips over there. Check in from time to time to see what I've added for you.

I'd love to hear more about your thoughts and experiences too. Who knows, your questions and comments might inspire me to write another book for you.

Come join me at: https://www.facebook.com/groups/playconnect/ I'll meet you there.

Brave Empathy

SOUVENIRS FROM MY FEELING WORD JOURNEY
What feelings have you noticed in the world? Add your own new words here.

Deborah Woods

ADVENTURES TO EXPLORE

List ideas to bring more comfortable feelings into your life.

Drake Baer, Why a Couples Therapist Says 'Emotional Fluency' Is Crucial for a Relationship: An Interview with Couples Therapist, Brian Gleason, June 29, 2016, thecut.com/2016/06/emotional-fluency-crucial-for-couples.html

Brené Brown, PhD, LMSW, Dare to Lead: Brave Work. Tough Conversation. Whole Hearts. 2018

Fredrickson, B. L. (2009). Positivity. New York, NY: Crown.

Sinclair, Shane, Beamer, Kate, Hack, Tom, McClement, Susan, Raffin Bouchal, Shelley, Chochinov, Harvey M and Hagen, Neil A. (2017) Sympathy, empathy, and compassion: A grounded theory study of palliative care patients' understandings, experiences, and preferences. Palliative Medicine, 31 (5). pp. 437447.

Deborah Woods

MEET YOUR TOUR GUIDE

"I look forward to the day when there's no longer a need for child therapists in the world. Until then, I'm going to keep bringing smiles and laughter to as many moms, dads, and kids as possible."

Deborah Woods, NCC, equips moms to raise happy kids, with great people skills, who grow up to be successful happy adults.

"Because the parent-child relationship is the best place for a child to grow, I created the Playtime Power Online Home Learning Program to help moms gain access to the wellspring of privileged information I discovered in my play therapy training. I'm excited that in the comfort of their own homes, parents are equipped to unleash joyful connection with their kids in just 30 minutes a week."

"I'm committed to helping moms and kids get the help that wasn't available to my family when we first needed it. Although the approach had been around in academic circles, it wasn't being shared widely enough to get to us. I am changing that."

Over the years, Deborah's expertise has been honored with a Master of Arts degree in Psychological Counseling, a board certification of National Certified Counselor and State of Missouri License in Professional Counseling. Deborah has spent over 15,000 hours playing with kids. In her Playtime Power Program Deborah teaches parents to have a 30 minute once a week playtime that uses the empathy, limit-setting, and child empowerment skills she uses in the office.

Deborah enjoys playing Guild Wars 2 with her son and his friends, visiting Laumeier Sculpture Park with family and friends, spending time watching Star Trek and John Wayne movies with her husband, attorney, David Woods, and making time for a strategic game of Settlers of Catan, or an exhilarating game of Munchkin with friends.

www.ingramcontent.com/pod-product-compliance
Lightning Source LLC
Chambersburg PA
CBHW040052160426
43192CB00002B/46